GENERATION E.D.G.E.

The Student's 4-Step Guide to College & Career Success

DR. JEN PRICE, LMSW

Generation E.D.G.E. Copyright © 2021 by UVISEME, LLC.

All rights reserved. Printed in the United States of America. No part of this book may be used or reproduced in any manner whatsoever without written permission except in the case of brief quotations embodied in critical articles or reviews.

No part of this publication may be reproduced or transmitted in any form or by any means, mechanical or electronic, including photocopying or recording, or by any information storage and retrieval system, or transmitted by email without permission in writing from the author.

Neither the author nor the publisher assumes any responsibility for errors, omissions, or contrary interpretations of the subject matter herein. Any perceived slight of any individual or organization is purely unintentional.

Brand and product names are trademarks or registered trademarks of their respective owners.

ISBN: 9781735836904

Book Design by Nkechi Obi

Cover Design by Pixel Studios

First Paperback Edition

For more information contact www.drjenprice.com

DEDICATION

This book is dedicated to my late parents, Kathy Jo and J.D. Houston, Jr. Both are no longer with me, but I know they are looking down from heaven cheering me on as I pursue a life of purpose. Thank you two for teaching me that learning is fun and critical to becoming successful. I know I pestered you both with tons of questions and constantly asked why. You can now chuckle because my son is the same way. He is also my motivation to be my best self. I pray that I can be the mother he needs me to be to embrace the greatness on the inside of him. (Son, I love you all day, every day…no matter what!)

I also want to thank my family members and friends who stood by me during my most difficult moments. I am eternally grateful for your unwavering love and support.

CONTENTS

NOTE TO READERS 3

INTRODUCTION 4

CHAPTER ONE 12
   As a Child

CHAPTER TWO 22
   Destination College

CHAPTER THREE 34
   A Major Dilemma

CHAPTER FOUR 54
   I've Got Skills

CHAPTER FIVE 75
   Final Thoughts/Words

CHAPTER SIX 82

Resources

Appendices 85
Appendix A..85
Appendix B..97

References 115

Acknowledgments... 116

About the Author 120

Also by Dr. Jen Price, LMSW 122

NOTE TO READERS

This publication reflects the opinions and ideas of its author. The intent of this book is to provide helpful and informative material on the subjects addressed. The strategies presented in this book may not be suitable for every individual. There is no guarantee or warranty to produce any particular results.

This book is sold with the understanding that neither the author nor the publisher is engaged in delivering college or career counseling, professional advice, or coaching services. The reader should consult directly with a competent professional before adopting any of the suggestions in this book or drawing inferences from it.

No warranty is made with respect to the accuracy or completeness of the information or references contained herein, and both the author and publisher specifically disclaim any responsibility for any liability, loss or risk, personal or otherwise, which is incurred as a consequence, directly or indirectly, of the use and the application of any of the contents of this book.

INTRODUCTION

What activities outside the classroom interest you—sports, marching band, student council, cheer, or youth group? Are you competitive? Do you simply enjoy being a part of the team, or are you after that medal, trophy, or championship? I enjoyed being a part of a team, but I also enjoyed winning the hardware.

When I first started running, I was in 8th grade. The season was short and was underway when my physical education teacher (and the track coach) saw me run in class. I was able to beat many of my classmates, called "PE Rangers" at the time. I had "potential" but was not properly conditioned. I reluctantly agreed to compete in the last few track meets of the season. My raw speed was only enough to place 5th in my heat at track meets. In my heart, I knew I could do better.

The summer before 9th grade, I decided I would train myself and continue running over the summer. At the time, I did not know about summer track programs or the Amateur Athletic Union (AAU). Nevertheless, I conditioned myself to run in the summer heat of Texas. I stretched, practiced drills, and ran 200-meter repeats. Some days, I practiced running a quarter mile, which is one lap around the track. When it rained, I would jump rope inside the garage at my house. I tried to eat healthier and cut sugary sodas out of my diet. I was committed and my daily habits reflected that commitment.

Long story short, my plan to improve in track worked. Freshman year, I was one of a few 9th graders invited to compete on the varsity team in the 1600-meter relay. Sophomore year, I was a part of a relay team that set a high school record in the 800-meter relay. (I think we still hold that record today.) Our relay team was invited to compete at the prestigious Texas Relays at The University of Texas at Austin—a meet where many of the world's fastest high school and professional athletes showcase their speed. During sophomore year, we also advanced to the state track meet and placed fourth despite a clumsy baton exchange between third and fourth leg. Throughout high school, I won many medals in the 200-meter dash, 400-meter dash, 400-meter relay, 800-meter relay, and 1600-meter relay. As a senior, I was named Sports Woman of the Year at my high school's annual banquet for my success and contributions on the track, in the classroom, and in the community. This achievement is something I am still proud of to this day.

Why am I sharing this story? Trust me, it is not just about reliving the "glory days." There were some lessons I stumbled across in my youth. These truths helped me succeed in sports, school, and later in my career. Allow me to share these truths; I believe they will help you too. With great humility and gratitude, I will share what I have learned to date as a college counselor, educator, entrepreneur, employee, sister, mother, and seeker of truth in Generation E.D.G.E., starting with the E.D.G.E. framework.

THE E.D.G.E. FRAMEWORK

The word E.D.G.E. is an acronym. Each letter represents a truth or aspect of the larger framework. The framework is outlined below and will reappear in the book with greater detail.

E-Explore and excel

D-Determine the best fit

G-Gain experience and skills

E-Evolve and emerge

Looking back, you can see I was applying the E.D.G.E. framework to my involvement in high school track. I tried a new sport and worked diligently to increase my endurance and speed (E-explore and excel). Despite my nerdy tendencies, I realized it would be helpful to participate in activities outside the classroom as well. I was not especially coordinated or experienced in many sports, but I could run fast. Therefore, I decided to compete in track and run cross country in offseason to maintain my endurance (D-determine the best fit). As I continued to train with upper classmen and the fastest sprinters on my team, I improved. Competing at track meets each year also helped me improve my form out of the blocks and during races. I learned how I needed to run the 400-meter dash without "dying" at the end (G-gain experience and skills). Although I decided against competing in track at the collegiate level, I did enjoy the occasional intramural race and tried new activities (E-evolve and emerge).

Other teens and young adults have followed my approach over the years, even before my methodology was officially labeled. Allow me a moment to thank all the football, basketball, soccer, and volleyball players, the golfers, artists, student leaders, cheerleaders, dancers, gymnasts, actors/actresses, singers, scientists, aspiring teachers, National Merit Finalists, valedictorians, and entrepreneurs who have given me an opportunity to sit with them and dream about their future.

Some of my favorite client memories to date:

- Valerie still holds the record for the most scholarship offers: $720,000.

- Maverick for being courageous to explore a career recommended during the career testing process. He had never heard of the major or the top college I recommended. Now he is finishing up a paid internship that has already turned into a job...PRIOR to graduation.

- Turning on the TV during football season and seeing former students marching in the band or cheering on the sidelines of a college football game.

- Matt for starting his real estate business while in college. I am so proud of you for executing on the plan we discussed when you were in high school. You have grown your real estate business and started a podcast. I am so excited and thankful for an opportunity to be on your show!

- The two female engineering students who turned down Columbia and Duke respectively to enroll in universities that were a better fit for each of them.

Many of my former clients have connected with me on LinkedIn. It is truly a joy to follow their career success.

I invite you to join my network as well: https://www.linkedin.com/in/jeniferprice/. Let me know you "met me" in my Generation E.D.G.E. book. You can also find me on social media (Instagram, Facebook, YouTube, and Twitter) @drjenprice.

WHAT TO EXPECT/BOOK OVERVIEW

This book is personal, practical, and strategic. It is written for you: teens, young adults, parents, and youth workers. However, many of the lessons apply to just about anyone seeking a fulfilling career.

In this book, I will share defining moments, both good and bad, from my life that helped me get to where I am today. Look out for cliff notes; these sections of the book highlight a practical life lesson for the reader. Finally, we will strategically apply the E.D.G.E. framework to your life in a way that allows you to create a plan for career success.

As a result of reading this book, you will:

- Have more fun in college because you are in a major that makes sense for you. Enjoy a more focused and fulfilling undergraduate or graduate school experience. No need to change your major 3 or 4 times, like your peers in college. You are more likely to graduate in fewer years if you are in the right major for you.

- Pay less for college because you have a career plan. Paying less for college may even mean fewer loans and more scholarships.

- Because you have a clear sense of what direction you are heading, you can start looking for and setting up a meaningful internship experience earlier in your academic career. Wouldn't a paid internship during your sophomore year be great?! Wouldn't it be even better if you had a job lined up *before* graduation?

- You can also scope out extracurricular activities and join organizations that will help you build your network socially and professionally.

CALL TO ACTION

I am convinced you were born for such a time as this. You are a gift to this world. There is only one like you. You are uniquely qualified to be you, and the way you can impact this planet and others is unique. Let's spend some time exploring what that might be.

Some of you may one day sway the social or political climate of the United States or the world through your song lyrics and beats. Others of you will conduct research in a lab to find ways to eradicate cancer. Maybe you are one who sees designs of flying cars in your dreams.

In this book, I will pose lofty questions about how you can add value through your vocation. While your career journey is your own, you are not alone. I am here to partner with you. I am here to join you in your quest to a fulfilling and impactful life. Consider me a guide. I am here to help you avoid some of the mistakes I made. Do not worry; you will still have ample opportunities to grow from any missteps you make in life.

I hope to encourage you and give you an opportunity to see the many possibilities your future holds. The advice and recommendations can potentially shorten your learning curve. Expect this book to inspire, educate, and empower. Let's do this!

CHAPTER ONE

As a Child

Whether it's how our parents raised us, how many siblings we have, our birth order, where we lived, where we went to school, or a childhood trauma, what happened during our childhood can impact the course of our life. Please allow me to share two impactful events from my childhood that have shaped the person I have become today.

Mothers impact our identity in profound ways. They lay that foundation of love and help us feel safe as we grow and explore what is in the world around us. They are there to nurture us with hugs, kisses, and reassuring words. I am grateful for the time I had with my mom and the lessons I learned from her. My experiences with my mother helped me be the strong woman, parent, counselor, educator, and entrepreneur I am today.

MY MOM

To this day, I can still remember waking to the sound of a dull thud. I was seven years old and one of my younger sisters, Holly, was five. Curious, my sister and I ran across the hall. Across the hall was our parents' room. The walls in their room were painted in a calming light blue with dark navy curtains framing each window. The king-size bed was empty. The vanity area in the master bathroom where my mom rolled her hair was also empty. This was odd.

Instead, I saw my mother lying on the floor motionless. My father was kneeling over her. He was on the phone calling for emergency medical assistance. My stoic, six-foot tall father was in full panic mode. I had never seen him so frantic.

At some point, my sister Kimberly, age two, joined us. I cannot recall where my five-month-old sister Jessica was during the commotion. As we waited for EMS to arrive, my sister Holly and I did the only thing we knew to do…pray. We prayed: "Lord, please don't let our mother die. Let her live!"

EMS arrived and kneeled over my mother. At first, I saw one EMT pressing down on her chest with both hands at reoccurring intervals. Later, they started placing two oval-shaped devices on my mother's chest. As a child, I did not know why they kept placing these devices on her chest. Apparently, the device made her body jerk. I now know they were trying to resuscitate her. However, I do not remember much of what happened next.

I only remember waking up in the guest room of my aunt's mobile home. On the wall of the guest room, I saw two certificates. I kept rereading them because I was confused. The same name and date was on both certificates. One looked like a birth certificate, but I did not know what the second certificate was for. To my knowledge, my aunt did not have a child. I did not have a cousin, or so I thought. I now realize my aunt lost her child immediately following birth. The second document was a death certificate. Little did I know I would soon become acquainted with that concept.

My aunt told my sister and me shocking news. She said my mother was no longer with us. She said my mother died. Being so young, it was hard for us to understand what she meant. At the time, my aunt did not offer much of an explanation. I did not understand the permanence of what she said, and I am sure my younger sisters understood even less. My mother was only 29 years old; she had died of a heart attack.

We sat on the front pew during my mother's funeral. The entire church was packed. There were no empty seats and many standing at the rear of the small church, unable to find a seat. My big, strong dad wept helplessly, and I hid behind him crying as well. Two of my sisters sat next to me refusing to shed a tear. I do not remember who was holding my five-month-old sister.

At the gravesite, we again sat on the front row of seats and watched her casket being lowered into the ground. I believed in my heart for many years my mom would one day return. We needed her; we needed a mother. However, she never returned.

No one ever really spoke to us about our mother dying. We never saw a counselor. My dad often said how much he loved and missed her. He even teared up at the thought of her absence. Somehow, the grief was never addressed; we simply moved forward with our lives. My dad went back to work. Two of us went back to school and the younger two went to daycare. This is when I decided it was time to be responsible. I no longer had time to play with Barbie dolls. As a big sister, it was time for me to watch out for my younger sisters.

Looking back upon my childhood, I now see how hurtful it was to miss out on those extra hugs, kisses, and reassurance from a mother. I forgot how to play. My self-sufficiency tendencies were activated at an early age. Choosing to develop a mindset of self-sufficiency at age seven meant I did not have to worry about whether someone was meeting my emotional needs. I even started to detach from how I felt and did not view life as something to be enjoyed. I was very afraid to depend on the love of others as it could suddenly disappear. Life was about achievement...in the classroom, on the track, and in the world of work. I unknowingly sought out all things resembling stability.

Although my mother never returned, I did come to terms with losing her later in life. I still carry with me many fond memories of our times together. Being the oldest, I remember her the most. I remember being her shadow, wanting to wash dishes and fold laundry with her. She instilled within me a love of learning and even taught me how to write in cursive before I started kindergarten. Because of her instruction, I often completed my assignments in class quickly once enrolled in school. I even helped my classmates along with their work so we could socialize. The funny thing is my son is now as chatty as I was in those days.

My mom always made sure we looked cute, from our hair bows to our lacey socks. Because of her, I love pizza, the color blue, and hosting parties, especially birthday celebrations. I am thankful she passed on the birthday tradition of cake, ice cream, and balloons. We kept the tradition after her death, and I continue to celebrate those I care about on their birthday. I joke about celebrating my birthday for the whole month of September; however, I am quite serious about finding ways to be thankful for another year of life.

Although she shared her creativity with the world as an artist and an interior designer, I have learned to express myself through the colors I wear and my words as a writer, coach, and speaker. Her entrepreneurial spirit is alive within me, as is a deep compassion for humanity. Like my mother, I have a mischievous streak and can be quite playful or feisty at times.

E.D.G.E CLIFF NOTE

The story of losing my mother may seem out of place in a book about preparing for your future. Let me explain. I know firsthand that one's upbringing can impact the ability to navigate the world and to build a healthy and happy life, but I also know this as a licensed social worker trained in counseling.

For those of you growing up without a mother, either through death or abandonment, I am sorry to hear of this happening to you. Perhaps you had a mother, but the relationship was harmful to you physically, mentally, or emotionally. Again, I hurt with you. Children need to grow up with a consistent nurturing force in their life. It is not your fault if you did not receive what you needed. Sometimes adults inadvertently or consciously make choices that impact their children in negative ways. Parents are human and imperfect.

If you have not taken time to grieve the loss of the mother you needed, I am giving you permission right now. I also recommend seeking help from a counselor in your school or at your university's health center. Early career adults can ask Human Resources if an Employee Assistance Program (EAP) exists; this benefit may help you identify a licensed and trained therapist to help you unpack the impact of this kind of loss on your life and possibly even on your career. You may also look online for a directory of licensed therapists that may be able to help as well. If money is a deterrent, ask if the therapist offers a sliding fee scale.

If you do have an overall positive association with your mother or with a caregiver in your life, please take a reading break and go give her or him a call or video chat. Do not simply send a text. A hug, if possible, is better. If you are currently at odds with this nurturing force (I get it; it happens), work through your issues if possible. Bring in a professional to help you if needed. Work through your childhood trauma. Your future self will thank you as you are able to fully embrace your destiny without baggage from your childhood.

SPEECH THERAPY

In elementary school, I lost my mother. I also started speech therapy. Each week, I was pulled out of class to meet with a speech therapist. My teacher said they could not understand what I was saying. She said I spoke too quickly. I spent an academic year running cards through a machine that taught me how to pronounce words…at a slower pace. What they did not know about me: I had SO many thoughts (including questions and ideas) running through my mind at any given time. It was difficult to release them all.

In junior high, I found an outlet for my many words. I decided to try theatre arts along with speech and debate. These were all great ways for me to express myself. Initially, I struggled with my presentation of poems, prose, and plays. With continued practice and the right pieces of literature and sometimes research, I learned how to construct a speech, memorize narrative, and convey emotion in presentations. I continued competing in speech and debate tournaments in high school. I even wrote speeches to apply for and win scholarships. There was even a time I used my oratorical skills to speak at a peace rally. By the end of high school, I had collected a lot of trophies, awards, and scholarships for an ability that was originally identified as a weakness and shortcoming.

The funny thing is, I still have tons of thoughts in my head at any given time. I now realize my words are like a superpower; I can use them for the good of others. My ability to use words have been an integral part of my career. My employment history is comprised of roles involving lots of words: teacher, software trainer, coach, author, and speaker.

E.D.G.E. Cliff Note

Sometimes your biggest weakness can become your superpower. Before you determine you are simply not good at something, work on developing that skill.

In what areas do you struggle? What can you do to develop that skill?

Write down your response.

E.D.G.E. Framework: E-Explore and Excel

The E stands for "explore and excel." I encourage you to explore your interests and abilities through extracurricular activities, which include clubs, sports, and community service.

The clubs and sports activities may be through the school or offered outside of school. Within a school, a student can participate in speech and debate club, student council, or art club. Outside of school, you may compete with a select sports team that may even travel.

Community service is work you do without pay; sometimes it is also called volunteer work. When you are volunteering, the work is generally for a nonprofit organization. Nonprofits are not trying to make more money than they use to run their organization. If you volunteer for an organization that is trying to make more money than they spend (a profit), you are probably not doing community service or volunteering. Keep track of the hours you volunteer for all organizations. Keep all the hours in one place. You may be able to use these hours on college applications, for scholarship consideration, or if you plan to join a sorority or fraternity in college.

Once you have figured out which activities are fun for you, it is time to do what you can to excel or improve your abilities. There are times when one-on-one lessons, extra classes, or camps can boost your performance, whether it is athletic, academic, or related to a specific skill. For example, some students play their sport year-round to get stronger and faster, or to develop better technique.

Homework Activity

Build a 4-Year Plan and an Activity List for High School or College.

Create a coursework plan for your four years in high school. Consult with your guidance counselor or college counselor if you have questions or want recommendations. Remember to discuss the appropriate level of rigor (on level, Pre-AP, AP) and which courses make the most sense for the college major/career you are considering at this time.

Additionally you will list the extracurricular activities you plan to participate in while in high school.

Download the sample 4-year plan and activity list (inclusive of a Community Service Log) plus the blank forms for high school and college at https://drjenprice.com/downloads

Start logging your volunteer hours the summer before 9th grade and through fall of 12th grade. Include hours spent working on projects with Girl Scouts or Boy Scouts and with churches or ministries.

    Extension Activity: Seek out advising support for course selection or coaching/consulting for help selecting extracurricular activities.

CHAPTER TWO

Destination College

Neither of my parents had a four-year degree. However, they both attended community college. My dad was able to earn an associate degree in applied science and a welding certificate. From what seemed like birth, I knew college was in my future. My parents and even parts of my extended family spoke of the importance of college. Despite their encouragement, I, like anyone, faced some challenging life circumstances and situations that threatened this dream.

My Dad

Despite having such a tragic childhood experience, I consider my life story one of resilience. I come from a place of forging ahead despite heartbreak, setbacks, and obstacles. I grew up in a single-parent home, raised by a widower.

My three sisters and I watched a man do everything. Our father kept the home spotless, learned how to cook, and even tried to figure out how to comb our hair. In addition to caring for four daughters, he managed to maintain the lawn, keep his vehicles washed, and drive us two hours away to visit our grandparents for a couple of hours on the weekend.

My sisters and I would essentially wait until we heard his pickup truck coming down the road to our house before we started to pick up any mess we had made…or to get rid of any evidence of questionable activity (like using the oven without permission) prior to his arrival. He changed clothes and immediately started preparing dinner.

Although there were times my father inadvertently burned the cornbread, his cooking skills improved over time. Baked chicken and cornbread were often on the menu along with some type of canned vegetable. Sometimes he would pick up a couple of frozen pizzas from the grocery store. Dinners were not fancy or elaborate, but Sundays after church were extra special. My father would mix up the menu a bit and always serve or prepare a dessert: Homemade ice cream, banana pudding, or cheesecake. (I have a sweet tooth just like my father!) By the time I was in high school, he had perfected his cornbread dressing recipe. We preferred his cornbread dressing over our grandmother's...on both sides of the family! My sister Holly has practically mastered his recipe, so spending Thanksgiving with her and her family is an extra special treat.

Every morning, my father prepared us a hot breakfast without fail. This is something I try to do for my son to honor the memory of my father. I cook him toast, biscuits, eggs (scrambled, scrambled with shredded cheese, fried, boiled, etc.), French toast, oatmeal, and more. Now that I am a parent, I understand how difficult it is to come up with meal ideas every day...and all day...now that my son is learning from home in the age of COVID.

My father believed in the power of education. He was highly supportive of our learning experience. I have many memories of him heading to the store to buy a poster board or two for presentations and projects. My father supported our interests and pushed us to excel and be involved in extracurricular activities and modeled service to the community. There were times when he would give a sister or me the last bit of cash he had for food while we were away with a club or team. Whatever we needed, he made sure we had it. He was a good man; I feel very blessed to have had that kind of upbringing.

My Dad's Visit with the Insurance Salesman

There was one evening I will never forget, one that forever changed the trajectory of my life. An insurance salesman met with my father in our home. My curiosity led me to listen to their conversation. The insurance salesman was trying to persuade my father to invest in life insurance. Apparently, the insurance would somehow help my father take out a loan to pay for my education.

The pitch did not make sense to me, and I, for whatever reason, offered my unsolicited input. I boldly declared the insurance was not needed because I would go to college on a full-ride academic scholarship. I was shocked to hear the insurance salesman's reply. He told me I would not be able to go to college on a full-ride academic scholarship; it was too difficult. In my mind, his response was ridiculous.

I do not recall if I protested or simply disengaged from the conversation. My father had already taught us all things were possible; there were no limits to what we could accomplish. He taught us to chase after our dreams...so I did. I devised a plan to win that full-ride academic scholarship for college and prove that salesman wrong.

E.D.G.E. Cliff Note

My father taught me there were no limits to what I could accomplish; I believed him. His confidence in me helped me set and chase after big dreams. Sometimes we need someone to believe in us and in the greatness that lies within. It can make a difference!

I learned another lesson: Do not let someone tell you what you cannot do. (English teachers, please excuse the double negatives.)

My Plan

I loved to learn and figured just about anything I needed to know could be found in a book. It seemed logical to involve the public library in my plan to find scholarships. Fortunately, my father started allowing my sister and me to spend hours at the public library on Saturdays. Between the card catalog and librarian, I was able to find many reference books with scholarship information. (I also discovered a new book genre: teen romance novels.)

After I wrote out contact information for numerous scholarship foundations, I started writing letters to request more information and applications. I started writing letters to scholarship foundations and programs…to request their applications. Then, I began asking my father for stamps to mail my letters. (When I was helping clean out my father's garage during the pandemic, I found one of my letters of inquiry. It is hard to believe I devised such a plan in 7th grade!)

First, I started a tickler file of scholarship opportunities to circle back around to in high school. Second, I reviewed the scholarship applications to learn what they were looking for in candidates…so I could become what they were seeking. I noticed the applications asked for grade-point average and sometimes coursework, including honors or Advanced Placement. The applications asked for sports, clubs, and extracurricular activity involvement along with leadership roles. It also asked about volunteer work and number of hours. Many asked for an essay. In some cases, the scholarship award was based on an essay or speech written on a specific topic. These applications were a roadmap for my high school experience. Looking back, I realize I essentially reverse-engineered the scholarship search process and simultaneously gained an edge in the admissions process by learning what kind of candidate I needed to become. What helped me be an ideal scholarship candidate also helped make me admissible to colleges.

In high school, my library research was helpful in an unexpected way. Not only did I learn about scholarship opportunities, but I discovered enrichment programs on college campuses across the country. When I was not busily working in my advanced-level courses and participating in sports, clubs, and service activities, I explored potential majors and college campuses. The career and college exploration was entirely accidental but lots of fun. (These experiences also helped me develop my E.D.G.E. framework.) I attended leadership, premed/biomedical, and honors programs at universities ranging from University of Texas at Austin, Texas A&M, Lamar University, and Florida A&M to name a few.

E.D.G.E. Cliff Note

Where there is a will, there is a way.

What do you want? How badly do you want it? If you want it badly enough, you can find a way to make it work.

I knew I wanted to go to college, but I did not know how to make this dream a reality. Through starting early, lots of research, reaching out for help along the way when needed, and diligence, I essentially reverse-engineered the college admissions process.

E.D.G.E. Framework: D-Determine the Best Fit

The D stands for "determine the best fit." I recommend career testing and building a list of prospective colleges or skills and training (a "learning list") needed to pursue your career interest area if a degree is not necessary.

Career Testing

Career testing is a great way to identify possibilities. It can also offer you some helpful insight. Depending on the career test or assessment, it may measure different things. While some measure your interests, others measure your aptitudes and abilities, or aspects of your personality.

You may already know what interests you. If you do not know what interests you, career testing can give you new ideas. However, looking at your interests alone is not enough to determine a career pathway. Maybe you enjoy basketball, but you are only 5 feet tall and cannot jump high. This is an example of having an interest but not the aptitude.

An aptitude is what you *can* do well. Again, looking at your aptitude or ability alone is not enough to determine a career pathway. What if you are good at writing poetry, but you have no interest in writing for a living? In this case, you have a high aptitude but low interest. It can be tough to pick a career to stick with long-term when you are good at it but do not enjoy it.

Some career tests recommend jobs or college majors based on your personality. The test may ask: Do you prefer being alone to recharge or are you more of an extrovert? While personalities vary, it still makes sense to look at your interests.

While some career testing is better than no career testing, I do recommend using a tool, if possible, that examines the overlap between interest, aptitude, and personality. This approach means the recommended careers are ones that you will enjoy, do well, and fit with your personality. Contact me if you need help finding one. I have used a career test for many years that has worked well with my individual clients. A conversation may also help you decide what type of job to pursue as you work toward building a career.

Homework Activity

After completing at least one career assessment, independently or with Dr. Jen Price, identify at least 3 career fields you may want to consider. Decide which college majors best align with your career goals.

Career Assessments

Free

- Texas Career Check's Interest Profile (previously Texas Cares) https://texascareercheck.com/ or https://texascareercheck.com/ExploreCareer/Interest Profiler

- Texas Reality Check

https://texasrealitycheck.com/

For a fee

- Strength Finder 2.0, Myers-Briggs, or testing with Dr. Jen Price, LMSW

Career Information

Occupational Outlook Handbook

Use this resource from the US Bureau of Labor and Statistics to research career options you are considering. Notice the level of education or training necessary to pursue this career. Learn more about working conditions, level of pay and more.

https://www.bls.gov/ooh/

Referencing two or three resources below, generate a list of up to 12 colleges that will meet your postsecondary needs and preferences (e.g., size, location, major, etc.). Include a range of institutions based on admissibility, grades, and test scores.

What are your top 5-8 colleges? Make sure you include a range of schools based on admissibility. Note whether a school is considered safer, a target, or reach option.

(A safer college is one where 75% or more of the students that apply are admitted. A target college admits 50-75%. A reach college admits less than 50% of the applicants.)

College Search Engines/Resource Guides

- Fiske Guide to Colleges by Edward Fiske

- College Board's Big Future

https://bigfuture.collegeboard.org/

- Peterson's College Search Tool

https://www.petersons.com/college-search.aspx

The Learning/College List

Learning is necessary for just about any job or career. There are times when learning is informal like on-the-job training at a grocery store or a fast-food establishment. Other times there are specific guidelines and timelines to learn and practice the skill, like in plumbing or becoming an electrician. Then, there are careers that require college, whether it is for a one-year certificate, a two-year, a four-year, or a graduate program. Regardless of the job or career, some type of learning is needed. However, all programs are not the same.

One college does not fit every student's needs. You may want to enroll in a community or junior college to "get some basics out of the way," but there is a bigger picture to consider. There are many questions to ask yourself when you are deciding which college is a best fit. What do you want to study in college? Some majors are stronger at certain schools. The size of the institution and most definitely the classroom can impact your ability to learn as well. Do you want your professor to know your name and notice if you miss class? Other questions to ask yourself include: How close or far away from home do you want to go? What kind of climate do you prefer? Are you planning to apply for a graduate or professional program after you earn your bachelor's degree?

If you feel overwhelmed at the idea of figuring out what you want, and more importantly, what you need to be successful in college, get help. As competitive as the college admissions process is now, you are at a disadvantage if you do not have help. Look for a college counselor with a background in counseling, preferably one who has worked with teens and young adults. Expect at least one graduate degree and possibly a license in counseling or some type of certification in college counseling. You want a counselor who visits college campuses and attends professional development activities on a regular basis. Because I have personally visited over 200 colleges across the U.S., I am able to bring a vast amount of knowledge to the college search process that others may not. I know firsthand it can be difficult to visit campuses working as a guidance counselor in a high school;

there are so many other administrative tasks to complete. I recommend supplemental support from an independent college counselor or from the use of a college advising tool.

When working with a private college counselor is cost prohibitive, I recommend seeking out an online college advising course that can take you step by step through the process. Check out College Edge (mycollegeedge.com); it has videos, a 45-page resource guide and homework activities designed to carry you through the college admissions process with less stress. You may also try conducting internet searches for what you need to know and read admission guidebooks. I will share some resources in this book. Reference Appendix A for campus visit tips.

CHAPTER THREE

A Major Dilemma

Because of my September birthday, I started kindergarten at age 6. Turns out, starting a year later meant I was fortunate to spend an extra year home with my mother the year before she unexpectedly died. I still remember to this day the pride I felt writing my name in cursive when I was in kindergarten. I also remember circulating the classroom and giving my peers the answers to questions so we would have more time to chat. I was in trouble with the teacher all the time because I talked too much. Some kids are just talkers...who grow up to be talkers...like me.

Why? Why not? As a child, I often questioned the reason for rules, decisions, and behaviors. I often asked for details. I was curious. I was so hungry for knowledge, I even read our family's set of World Book Encyclopedias. Then, I would sit my younger sisters down and teach them what I had learned. I loved learning and the idea of going to a place dedicated to learning—school. Honestly, there were signs that I would later become an educator, but no one saw the writing on the wall.

In many families, student majors are predetermined by family expectations. In certain cultures, the range of acceptable career options may be limited. As family members observed my thirst for knowledge and learned of my academic prowess, I was encouraged to consider prestigious careers such as medicine or even law. What's funny to me was no one ever asked if I especially enjoyed science.

Medicine

I'm not sure if my father was knowingly assisting me in my career exploration efforts, but he regularly supported my interests in attending weekend and weeklong summer enrichment programs regionally and across the country. Texas A&M offered a summer medical program for high school students, which allowed us to become better acquainted with the field and career pathway. We were even given an opportunity to stay on a college campus, which was very exciting.

Ultimately, I ruled out a career in medicine after my field trip to Herman Hospital in Houston, Texas. My AP Biology classmates and I viewed a cadaver. It was an older man; he appeared to be someone's grandfather. I am not trying to gross anyone out, but they had sliced his body into four quarters. We viewed the top half of his body, which was again cut in half. The outside and inside of his body could be viewed depending on the side one stood. I was cool, calm, and collected as I looked at his bones, organs, and tissue. However, when I saw his face and thought about those he left behind, I began to fall apart. What I didn't realize at the time was my compassion for humanity; I didn't know I had the heart of a counselor. I only knew I wanted to help others in some way.

Law

My best subjects in school involved reading, discussion (aka talking), and writing, so there was more of a case for the pursuit of law. Plus, I was on the speech and debate team starting in junior high, and I continued with this extracurricular activity through high school. I often argued with my father, sometimes late into the night when my sisters simply wanted to go to bed. I remember pleading with him to just see the good in people. My dad, on the other hand, was simply trying to prepare me for a world that struggles to maintain justice. Although my dad did his best to shelter me from the racism in our community, he didn't want me blindsided by the discrimination Blacks regularly faced in our small town and in our country.

Not until we were clearing out my dad's home and sorting through old newspaper clippings, letters, and cards did I remember that I was spotlighted in the local newspaper for speaking to our community about the importance of unity. Again, there were signs of me being a talker and wanting to make an impact on others by motivating them to treat others fairly. I'm not sure why a career in law fell off the radar. In retrospect, it might have been a great fit for me. Perhaps my waning interest in speech and debate in my later years of high school contributed to not pursuing this pathway. I'm not sure. What I do remember is the high regard held for careers in science.

Pharmacy

Although I decided against medicine, I started to consider another option in the healthcare field: pharmacy. The decision to pursue this field of study was based on logic. In 10th grade, we researched careers related to chemistry. I learned that pharmacists didn't have to go to school as long as doctors, but they were paid well. Plus, I knew my family members would approve of this option. As a part of my research project in my chemistry course, I shadowed a pharmacist for 10 hours.

When I was old enough (16), I even applied to work as a cashier in the same pharmacy. Truth be told, I wasn't really interested in counting pills or advising patients on drug interactions. I especially didn't enjoy elderly patients cursing me out when I told them they were out of refills on their controlled substances (e.g., codeine). (Please note: All pharmacists don't dispense medication in a retail setting. There are other ways they serve. At the time, this was all I knew.)

I was highly driven by the prestige and money associated with becoming a pharmacist. Honestly, you should look it up on the Occupational Outlook Handbook. Google it and locate the salary. For these reasons, I focused my college search on institutions in Texas with pharmacy programs. Although I could have attended another college and applied for pharmacy school after a couple of years, I wanted to stay in one place the entire time. University of Texas (UT) was my #1 choice because I heard from my aunt that my late mother had always wanted to attend this university. If you've ever seen the movie Jerry McGuire, they also "showed me the [scholarship] money!"

Although I excelled academically in high school, I quickly learned that my peers at UT were also competitive in the classroom. Imagine attending school with the best and brightest from your high school. My freshman year, I experienced test anxiety and sought help from the learning center. I also learned how important it was to keep up in class. Consuming massive amounts of information in a short period of time (e.g., cramming) is much more difficult in college than in high school...no matter how smart you are.

Organic Chemistry

For those of you already in college, I know you've heard about the course Organic Chemistry. Well, this course changed my life in many ways. I took Organic Chemistry I three times! The first time, I took it in summer school and realized I had bit off more than I could chew and dropped it. The second time I took it, I earned a D and was required to retake it. (Let me just add, I attended every lecture, lab, and supplemental instruction class available. I bought molecular models and went to tutoring...in fact, I studied so much for this course, my eyes were often bloodshot.) The third time I took the course, I was grateful to earn a C and advance to Organic Chemistry II. I was determined to work my plan; I refused to be dissuaded from a career in pharmacy.

I enrolled in Organic Chemistry II. I took this course twice! I was still miserable. It felt like I was banging my head against a wall...and my head was bleeding! One day, it occurred to me I could attend college and take courses that I actually enjoy. This was the catalyst for seeking out help at the career center on campus. I learned that career assessments could help me identify a major that better fit my interests and abilities.

Career Testing Saves the Day

Results confirmed social sciences and helping professions were a better fit...majors like sociology, social work, and education were a fit. Again, I thought about what I really wanted in a career: a way to help people. I carefully weighed my options based upon A-L-L the science courses I had taken. Upon looking at degree plans, I realized I could still graduate in close to four years (four years and a full summer session to be exact). My exit strategy involved switching from a pre-pharmacy major in the college of natural sciences to liberal arts. On the last day of add/drops for spring courses in the final few minutes, I successfully enrolled in coursework for my new major in sociology. My new career plan was to minor in social work, a field I had never heard of, and later apply to a master's degree in social work.

My family was epically disappointed. I suddenly felt like the black sheep in my family. Not only did I forsake a career field in the sciences, but I selected a major with low prestige and one associated with low-income levels. It took me years to stop worrying about other people's opinions of my degree. What mattered most was that I had chosen a path that best suited me.

During the world-wide pandemic of 2020, counseling has received much needed recognition for the value it brings to society. There has been a high demand for counselors of all types. Individuals and families have sought out support in the areas of marriage, social isolation, anxiety, depression, career, and more.

E.D.G.E. Cliff Note

As Shakespeare says, "To thine own self be true." Listen to YOUR gut; it will help you avoid heartache and detours. Don't choose your career based on what others think. You are the one who has to live with the decision. Choose a career based on YOUR interests, aptitudes, and personality. Develop a career plan that takes income into consideration.

E.D.G.E. Framework: G-Gain Experience and Skills

The G stands for "gain experience and skills." Once you have identified a couple of possible career options that suit you and enroll in a postsecondary institution where you will thrive, it is time to start thinking about ways to gain work experience and to develop your skillset. Starting to connect with prospective employers sooner versus later is essential. Do not wait until graduation from college or completion of your career training program to look for job opportunities. There are several ways you can connect with other professionals in fields you are considering.

Information Interviews

As a part of the career testing process, I suggest you contact individuals who are in careers you wish to explore. Asking for an information interview is a great way to initiate a conversation. An information interview is time set aside to ask another person about their job or career. You ask for a chance to meet and ask about their work. It is important that you write your questions out in advance. I often tell my students more seasoned adults simply love talking about themselves and what they know.

Setting up a conversation can be easy if you begin with those within your network. Your network of contacts start with who you know: family members, immediate and extended; friends and their parents; educators: school administrators, teachers, coaches, or guidance counselors; church leaders and members; neighbors; or anyone you interact with on a regular basis. Career service departments are a great source for college students. At times, I have asked students to conduct research and to identify potential people to cold call. When I say cold call, I mean calling and/or emailing an individual to request an interview with the hope of scheduling a time to talk. Again, most people like to talk about themselves and are happy to chat with you...over the phone, via videoconference, or in person at their office or in a coffee shop.

What is important to remember is an information interview is not the same thing as a job interview. However, it may lead to one in the future or even to an internship. This is what happened to one of my former clients. She was interested in veterinary medicine. It all started with an information interview with one of her mother's friends. The conversation led to a paid internship, something I will talk about a bit later.

Job Shadow

Another way to learn about a job or career is to request or set up a job shadow. A job shadow involves observing someone working in their office at their place of employment. Seeing tasks completed in the work environment provides tremendous insight into a job. When I was considering a career in pharmacy, I shadowed a retail pharmacist for 10 years. It helped me to see what it was like standing on your feet for long hours, dispensing or compounding medication, and handling customers who were ill or in pain. I will never forget being cursed out by an elderly customer for informing her the prescription with codeine she was trying to refill did not have any more refills. Over the years, my clients have observed architects in action on a job site, an executive vice president in luxury retail, and even a coroner trying to determine the cause of death.

Volunteer vs. Intern

Volunteers do not receive pay for the work they do. Interns may or may not receive compensation depending on the position (e.g., paid or non-paid internship). Another difference between being a volunteer and an intern is the type employer you assist. Volunteers work for organizations that are not seeking a profit. Any money they collect is to cover the cost of serving others and operating the organization. Conversely, internships tend to include businesses; the mission of a business is to generate profits (e.g., make money). There are some businesses that prioritize social issues or give back part of their profits to the community.

Whether it is volunteer work or an internship, you will have an opportunity to gain exposure to a career field that potentially interests you. While I was in high school, I volunteered to teach children lessons about life. In college, I mentored a child for a semester. By the time I was in graduate school, I completed a placement at high school facilitating groups for pregnant teens and another one at a charter high school's career resource center. I didn't realize what I was doing at the time, but I was figuring out how much I enjoyed working in education and with students.

To be competitive in the college admissions process or job hunt, list volunteer work (or community service) AND at least one internship on your resume. Your resume is a summary of your involvements and accomplishments. It is not typically longer than two pages. High school students can ask a parent or guidance counselor for help putting this document together. College students may seek out their career services department for sample resumes, coaching, and workshops. An independent college counselor or online resources can also help with this task.

Employment

An internship is generally short-term and centered around learning; however, employment is work one does for pay. The job may be on a temporary, part-time, or full-time basis. Jobs can confirm or deter you from a career field. Working part-time at a nationwide pizza chain taught me I wanted a better work schedule and much higher pay. I saw firsthand the struggle of fellow employees with a high school diploma trying to live on their income as delivery drivers or cooks; it was tough! Some even had families they were struggling to support. The managers earned higher wages, but still worked evenings and weekends, which were the times I wanted to spend with family or friends.

Homework Activity: Build an Extended Resume

Create an expanded resume using the resources provided. Consider using the formatting of a resume template in a word processor as a starting point. Include as many details as possible. The more detailed your resume, the easier it will be to fill out your college applications.

Reference the resume guidelines and action verbs in this book. Select a suitable action verb as you describe your level of participation in clubs, service activities, and on athletic teams.

Reference Appendix B for sample resumes.

Extension Activity: Ask a professional to review your resume and offer constructive feedback. Consider enrolling in Dr. Jen's online course College Edge to access the portfolio checklist. The portfolio is documentation of all that you have participated in and accomplished throughout your years in school. It includes standardized test score reports, certificates of achievement, a community service log, and more.

Resume Guidelines & Action Verbs

Resume Guidelines

- Standard business font (i.e., Arial, size 11 or 12; or Times New Roman, size 12)

- Length of resume: 2 pages or less typically, but expanded resumes may be up to 4 or 5 pages

- Phrases instead of sentences

- Each statement begins with a strong, active verb

- Specific examples and numbers to show measurable accomplishments

- "I" and "me" omitted

- Perfect grammar, spelling, and punctuation

- Pleasant to the eye (i.e., simple design elements, enough white space)

Action Verbs for Accomplishment Statements

- Accelerated

- Accomplished

- Achieved

- Administered

- Analyzed

- Approved

- Budgeted

- Built
- Completed
- Conceived
- Conducted
- Consolidated
- Controlled
- Converted
- Coordinated
- Created
- Cut
- Delegated
- Delivered
- Demonstrated
- Designed
- Developed
- Devised
- Directed

- Doubled
- Earned
- Edited
- Eliminated
- Established
- Evaluated
- Expanded
- Forecast
- Formulated
- Generated
- Headed
- Implemented
- Improved
- Improvised
- Increased
- Installed
- Invented

- Innovated
- Instituted
- Introduced
- Launched
- Led
- Maintained
- Managed
- Motivated
- Negotiated
- Organized
- Originated
- Operated
- Performed
- Planned
- Presented
- Processed
- Produced

- Programmed
- Promoted
- Proposed
- Provided
- Purchased
- Recommended
- Recruited
- Redesigned
- Reduced
- Reorganized
- Researched
- Revised
- Scheduled
- Serviced
- Set Up
- Simplified
- Sold

- Solved
- Sparked
- Staffed
- Started
- Streamlined
- Strengthened
- Stressed
- Stretched
- Structured
- Succeeded
- Summarized
- Superseded
- Supervised
- Systematized
- Terminated
- Traced
- Tracked

- Traded
- Trained
- Transferred
- Transformed
- Translated
- Trimmed
- Tripled
- Uncovered
- Unearthed
- Unified
- Unraveled
- Utilized
- Vacated
- Verified
- Widened
- Withdrew
- Won

- Worked
- Wrote

CHAPTER FOUR

I've Got Skills

Not many can say they landed their dream job right out of college. I can, but it took a lot of forward thinking. This is how it happened.

Studying Sociology

As I mentioned before, career testing ultimately saved me from the misery of Organic Chemistry II. It helped me decide to major in sociology at the undergraduate level and social work at the graduate level. As a liberal arts major (in sociology), I started feeling excited about school again. Attending class was no longer a chore. I was more easily able to grasp the concepts taught to me in class; it seemed more intuitive. The subject intrigued me...especially as the topic intersected with education. My grades shot up; I went from academic probation and the threat of losing my full-ride scholarship to the Dean's List for earning all A's and one B. What was even more miraculous was the fact that I could still graduate in four years and summer school after changing my major in the middle of my junior year in college.

Studying Social Work

I only had a two-week break between earning my bachelor's degree and starting a master's program in social work. I wish I could say I enjoyed studying social work. While I found it incredibly fascinating to learn about lifespan development (e.g., infancy, childhood, adolescence, early adulthood, middle age, older age) and counseling techniques, I really struggled with sharing aspects of my perspective in class.

I found it easier to share about the ways I had experienced unfair treatment as a female and a minority. At my first job, I was sexually harassed by my superior. He repeatedly made inappropriate sexual remarks and found ways to brush up against my body no matter how much effort I made to stay away from his. When this was reported by my female coworker and me, our boss was reprimanded and simply reassigned to another store. (I do not understand how this kind of disrespect and improper conduct is tolerated in work environments, and I am deeply disturbed that other females have experienced this and more.)

Most of the time, I was the only Black in my honors and Advanced Placement courses in high school. Therefore, attending a university with only 3% Black students (out of a student body of 50,000) was not a new experience. Despite growing up in a community known at one time for racism, college is where I encountered blatant racial hatred. First, there were heated conversations about affirmative action with peers. Then, came the assertions that I didn't belong at our state's flagship university or deserve an academic scholarship when I was ranked in the top 2% out of over 400 other students in my high school. On another occasion, I saw "Nigger go home" spray painted in the elevator at my dorm. These experiences pale in comparison to my Uncle Lonnie Fogle's experience at University of Texas of Austin decades earlier. As one of the first Blacks to attend my undergraduate alma mater, my uncle wasn't even allowed to live on campus. Because of his many peaceful protests with peers and the many others committed to equity, I along with other Blacks, including those from our family, were able to attend.

While in my master's program, I felt pressured to speak for my entire race at times. Truth is...there is so much diversity within the Black community: varying family structures, a range of socioeconomic backgrounds, differing political perspectives, and more. My peers and professors seemed to embrace me as a Black female.

What I wasn't prepared for was the discrimination I faced for my religious views. In general, social workers are known for embracing differences, whether it is based on race, gender, sexual orientation, or faith. Considered the dominant faith at that time, Christianity was often criticized or barely addressed. During classroom conversations, I recall feeling like the only one brave enough to share their convictions as a Christian when other non-Christians shared what *they thought* the faith espoused. Other Christians would come up to me after class and practically whisper a thanks for sharing the viewpoint of a Christian. Simple stated, they were afraid of being ostracized or labeled intolerant.

Time and time again, I presented the truth of the God I serve, one who is loving of all people. It pains me that religiosity and legalistic churches have shamed more than loved others regardless of where they are in life. Furthermore, I am thankful to have a blueprint (the Bible) and a role model (Jesus Christ) to help me make decisions about life and to offer me a set of guidelines that doesn't constantly change based on the whim of another man. For example, I am encouraged to genuinely love others (e.g., my neighbor) as I love myself. This approach involves acknowledging the value of others and ourselves.

My First Job

My first job out of college was the result of my graduate studies in social work. In the final semester of my master's program in social work, all students were required to intern on a full-time basis at an area nonprofit. Because I knew I wanted to eventually become a college and career counselor, I sought out school-based social work opportunities. After researching area nonprofits and charter schools, I identified one that had a college and career center and an employee with a master's in social work. I was essentially able to create my own field placement with an organization that would help me begin my career in college and career advising. About six weeks into my field placement, I was able to interview for a position in that department. Score! This made me one of the few social work students able to earn a full-time salary as I completed my degree. Within a year, I was the Career Center Coordinator, managing up to 10 people during the summer youth employment program.

What I Learned

I learned several lessons from that first job. First, I learned how important research is. Study yourself. You need to know yourself and what you want so you can find the kind of work environment that is a fit for you. The fit may be about helping you gain the skills you need to start out your career or to expose you to the type of position you think you want. Explore the range of employers in your area of interest. Do they offer internships? Are they hiring? Are any of the positions at entry level? How are the employers similar and different? Does one employer seem like more of a fit for you based on where you are in your career? Asking all these questions and finding an answer through research helped me land an internship that turned into a full-time job.

Second, I learned opportunities are often for those who are willing to step outside their comfort zone. As I stated before, I was promoted into a management position after a year of working at my first job. I was the youngest in my department and had the least amount of experience. However, I was willing to step outside my comfort zone and actually apply for the coordinator position. It felt awkward to supervise the woman who trained me when I started, but I was willing to take on the challenge of leadership. My communication skills definitely grew, and I started learning the importance of empowering your employees through delegation.

Third, I learned how important my convictions are. Honesty and integrity are very important to me. I try to say what I mean and do what I say. Have I ever failed to do what I believe or say? Yes. However, I strive daily to live a life of congruence, a life where my beliefs and actions are in alignment. Anytime you have a belief, I can guarantee you will be tested. As I was reporting data for a report, I received indirect pressure to adjust the number for the sake of maintaining grant funding. However, I was not comfortable compromising. In fact, I ultimately decided to walk away from a position instead of choosing to be dishonest. The decision was a tough one to make. I did not have a backup plan, but I was married at the time. We lived well within our means, so my decision did not create a financial crisis. Plus, we both graduated without any student loan debt. Within five weeks, I was able to start a new job earning 50% more than the previous position! When we do what is right, I do believe things can work out in the end.

Technology Startups/DotComs

Working at a technology start up or dotcom was all the rage back in the early 2000s. I'm sure others, like me, had dreams of becoming rich like the Dellionaires of the late 1990s. I learned many lessons working in a fast-paced, entrepreneurial environment. Some of the lessons were more painful than others.

What I Learned

First, I learned I was not as driven by money. This was ironic because I sought out this kind of employer for the financial gains, yet that is not what largely motivated me. I found myself working long and at times odd hours to accommodate customers across the globe (4 am or even Sundays). There were days I would cry during my lunch break because I was so miserable as a result of my job.

My main takeaways from this experience: You need to listen to your gut. If it doesn't feel right to you, no matter how much money you earn, it isn't worth it in the end.

I gained quite a bit of weight due to the stress I experienced while working at my first technology start-up. It also caused quite a bit of stress in my relationships outside of work.

Second, I learned that everyone doesn't prioritize authenticity and transparency as much as I do. In the technology sector, it's not uncommon for products to release with known bugs. Coming from a background in education and counseling, I did not know this would become a source of stress for me. Customers would complain about shortcomings with functionality, and I felt blindsided at times.

In some cases, I was told a bug was fixed, but the customer had a different experience. This is when I learned that some people are not as transparent. Ego can drive some to misrepresent truth and to say things that are simply not true. It still confuses me when some people are not willing to own their mistakes.

The takeaway here is to be aware of your work environment and the type of people you may encounter in a particular industry. Internships are key to preparing you for the workforce.

Believe it or not, I had the audacity to work at a second technology start-up...one that was like the first. I wanted to accelerate paying off my luxury SUV. Let me first acknowledge, I did not need such a large vehicle just for me. Maintenance was expensive, and it drank gasoline like water. I placed myself in yet another highly stressful environment to enjoy a material possession. Again, I learned the risk was not worth the benefit.

The takeaway here: Don't be in a hurry to buy your dream car, truck, or SUV out of college. As your earnings increase, invest in appreciating assets first like a duplex, condo, a townhome, or a house.

Back to School

They say hindsight is 20/20. In retrospect, I could have committed to the pathway of becoming a public-school educator and counselor. I could have earned my bachelor's degree and teacher's certificate and entered the classroom immediately following graduation. After a year or two, I could have started a master's program in counseling to work towards my school counselor designation. Another ambitious step would have been to earn my mid-level management certificate or to pursue a role as a principal. However, I didn't. I chose the path I thought would lead me in the most direct path to independent college counseling.

Right out of college, I knew what I wanted to do for my career, but I needed professional experience. At least, I had an inkling of what I didn't know. I realized that what I had learned about the college admissions process and career exploration process were anecdotal and unique to my circumstances. Working in a charter school and in a traditional public school as a teacher and a private school as a college counselor for just under 10 years gave me important insight. Not only did I learn about the differences between school settings, but I also gained insight into their strengths and shortcomings in serving students. More specifically, I learned how each system addressed the college and career advising needs of their students and families.

While schools and districts differ, my background in school settings helped me to develop an effective approach to college and career advising in my private practice. I know where the schools fall short in helping families. I bring an awareness of these shortcomings to the process I offer in my one-on-one college counseling appointments, and subsequently in my online course College Edge. There are a couple of major challenges students in school settings face when it comes to navigating the college admissions process. First, the caseloads in schools can be quite large. The American School

Counselor Association (ASCA) collects data on counselor-to-student ratios. At the time of this printing, the national average is 430:1. I have even met counselors from states such as New York with over 800 students on their caseload! While a private school counselor's caseload may be smaller (e.g., 75 to 100), these administrators generally juggle additional campus-wide responsibilities outside of college advising. Second, I also remember how difficult it was to leave campus for an admission update from a college or to fly out to a university-sponsored campus visit. However, independent college counselors regularly visit campuses as an integral part of their job. To date, I have been able to visit over 200 colleges. Admissions requirements are constantly changing, and the process is becoming more selective. Staying up to date with admissions trends is essential to helping students gain a competitive edge.

Teaching the equivalent of career prep courses in grades 6th-12th and counseling high school students in different school settings also helped me figure out how to best guide students in their career search. I learned that all school settings struggle with selecting a career assessment tool that is accurate and able to reliably predict suitable careers for a student. It is difficult to find one that can be widely administered to its student body with ease and little disruption to the learning environment. Another common problem is the results are not always easy to digest. Families are often overwhelmed with the many options presented to them. They really need to sit down with someone and talk through the recommended career options. Also needed is independent time to review career options and information about these careers (e.g., education/training pathway, work environment, salary, etc.). Talking with individuals already in the student's field of interest is another effective way to research careers.

As the number of client families started to increase in my independent college counseling practice, I knew I would at some point run out of bandwidth. I struggled for years with identifying a way to scale in a way that worked for me. I tried communications interns to help with social media and administrative tasks. I partnered with a graduate program in education to help me develop instructional material for my clients. I hired a phone answering company. I even considered adding other counselors to my practice. In this midst of trying different approaches to scale, I instinctively knew online learning was the next wave in education. This led to me exploring PhD programs in education.

Ultimately, I decided I wanted to learn more about how we learn and to create a tool that would teach even more students and families what I know about the college admissions and career selection process. Once again, I used my research skills and figured out the name of what I wanted to learn. I explored programs across the country and found one that offered primarily live synchronous instruction to feel a sense of community and instate tuition rates while studying at a distance. I am grateful to have had the opportunity to return to school to earn my PhD in education with a concentration in instructional design and technology. The process was way more difficult than I could have ever imagined. Through diligence, help at home, and a very supportive advisor, I was able to endure and complete my PhD journey. What I learned about distance and online learning from experience, textbooks, and my dissertation laid the groundwork for my online college advising course College Edge (mycollegeedge.com). I can agree with the saying, all things work together for the good!

E.D.G.E. Cliff Note

Trying different things can teach us important lessons. As it relates to the world of work, trying different working environments or roles in an organization can show us where we thrive and where we don't. Learning what isn't a fit is important information.

Opportunity is all around you. Sometimes it's about seeing a need and devising a way to fill it. Through working in education, I gained knowledge, skills, and experience. I also learned from what wasn't working. Shortcomings can become opportunities.

E.D.G.E. Framework: E-Evolve and Emerge

The second E in the framework stands for "evolve and emerge." You will likely embark upon this phase after a couple of years of employment. It tends to happen three to ten years into your career. For some, it comes when they determine something is "missing" in their career. To evolve, assessment and alignment are necessary. You then emerge as action is taken on your plan.

Evolve

To evolve, it is helpful to assess where you are currently in your career and to determine if you are in alignment with your definition of career success.

Evolve, Part I: Assessment

As you gain experience and skills working in your early years, notice the areas you seem to gravitate towards. Have most of your jobs been in a particular industry (e.g., nonprofits, technology, healthcare, customer service, or hospitality)? What aspects of each job do you enjoy most: crunching numbers, resolving issues for customers or clients, managing a team, or something entirely different? Answering these questions and others will help you identify patterns in your employment history and possibly insight into what direction you may want to head next.

If you look at my work history on LinkedIn, you will notice my ongoing interest in educating and advising others. In a school setting, this looked like being a teacher or counselor at the secondary level. In a startup environment, this was a technology support or training role. Most of the roles I gravitated toward involved serving teens and young adults as well as their families.

Evolve Activity, Part I (Assessment)

Answer the following prompts:

1. Describe the kind of industries you have worked in. Which industries have been most appealing to you?

2. What kind of skills do you find yourself using over and over?

Evolve, Part II: Alignment

According to the Merriam-Webster Dictionary, alignment is defined as the act of aligning or the state of being aligned especially: the proper positioning or state of adjustment of parts in relation to each other. In this book, alignment is about you being in the proper career, one that is a fit for your experience, skill set, interest, values, and personality. There are many facets to who you are and many ways for you to contribute to society.

It is not uncommon for someone to work in a field because they are good at it. Like I tell my clients, just because you are good at math that does not automatically mean you should be an engineer. There are other career fields suitable for people who "get" math: financial advisor, auditor, computer programmer, statistician, or even a data/research analyst.

As I volunteered and worked part-time jobs with the university as a college student, I learned how much I enjoyed serving teens and young adults. During my junior year in college, a course on career exploration helped me determine what kind of work I wanted to do with teens and young adults.

Evolve Activity, Part II (Alignment)

Answer the following prompts:

1. Think of your favorite job to date. What aspects of the job energize you most?

2. What does your dream job look like? Write a job description and list the experience and skills needed. What is your work schedule? What does the work environment look like? How much do you earn?

3. It may be helpful to work with a career coach or counselor as you figure out the answers to these questions and more, especially if you "get stuck" or lack clarity.

Emerge

The final E in the E.D.G.E. framework represents "evolve and emerge." You emerge or become a more prominent professional in your field by mapping out a plan for career success and taking action.

Emerge, Part I: Employment or Entrepreneurship

Depending on your current level of satisfaction with your career, you may decide to stay where you are, transition to another position or organization, or create your own business.

Emerge Activity, Part I: Employment or Entrepreneurship

Purchase a journal or start a new document in a word processor (e.g., Microsoft Word or Google document). You now have a designated place to craft a career that best suits you. Depending on your desired outcome, you may choose to pursue employment or entrepreneurship. Answer the prompts for the direction you are heading currently. If you plan to work a while until you transition into entrepreneurship, complete both sections.

Option A: Employment

Answer the following prompts:

1. Once you have greater clarity regarding what you want in your career, decide if what you are seeking already exists.

    (a) Do these positions exist? If so, apply for these positions.

    (b) If not, you may need to revise your resume and focus on the skills (e.g., transferable skills) needed for a new position.

2. Research and apply for some of those types of positions. Start with your university's career center, alumni association, or LinkedIn. Job boards like Indeed, ZipRecruiter, and Monster are great places to look as well.

You may also consider seeking the help of a professional resume writer, career coach, or headhunter.

If you realize what you are seeking is not already out there, you may want to consider taking what you already know and creating the kind of position you desire.

Option B: Entrepreneurship

Answer the following prompts:

1. Is there a way to use what you already know to generate income? In your journal, make a list of what you know a lot about (e.g., teaching/training, managing others, writing code, etc.). List your strengths as well.

2. If you are looking for reassurance or searching for new ideas, take a career assessment or revisit career assessment outcomes. Are there any options you would like to explore? If so, which ones?

3. Write a business plan and decide how you will transition into this new venture. If you need help with your plan or with putting together a timeline, seek out a career and/or business coach. Working with a coach may require an investment, but the investment shortens your learning curve to profitability.

Resources for Entrepreneurs

I used several free and low-cost resources locally, statewide, and nationwide to aid me in my journey towards entrepreneurship. You can too! Below are some places I found support.

1. Books: I visited my local library, discount bookstores, and shopped online for books about writing business plans, marketing, and other related topics.

2. Workshops and Classes: I was able to enroll in workshops and classes with the City of Austin, the Small Business Association (SBA) and their resources for women, Business Invest in Growth (BiG Austin), and Professional Women of Williamson County (PWOW). SCORE offered free mentoring from seasoned entrepreneurs.

3. Colleges: Community colleges and area universities may offer programs or courses. My senior year in college, I took an independent study course with Dr. John Sibley Butler of the University of Texas at Austin on Blacks and entrepreneurship. His course allowed me to create the foundations of what later became my college and career advising business.

4. I also took courses at Austin Community College (ACC), Texas State University's ACTiVATE program for female entrepreneurs, and a startup program through Rice University (Rice Alliance) that ended

with an opportunity to pitch your business idea to venture capitalists.

5. Professional and Trade Associations: You may also be able to connect with a professional or trade association that offers self-employment support. I joined Independent Educational Consultant Association (IECA). They offered a summer institute. IECA also offers numerous professional development opportunities (e.g., a listserv for questions, a local networking group, monthly newsletters, two conferences a year with college visit opportunities). I also took coursework from a certificate program in college counseling at University of California Los Angeles's Extension Program.

6. Business Coaches: I am currently coaching a limited number of entrepreneurs. However, I can refer you out to a reputable coach if needed.

Emerge Part II: Action

Action demands intentionality. You cannot half-heartedly attempt to execute on your plan. Saying you will try is not enough; you have to decide to be committed to living a life that is purposeful and fulfilling. Being a game-changer also means consistency. To be consistent, daily habits are necessary. The choices you make every day turn into habits and ultimately determine how successful you will or will not be in your career.

Intentionality is necessary when you are mapping out a plan for career success. Not only did I want to help teens and young adults with career exploration, but I decided college selection played an important role in designing one's roadmap to a best-fit career. Junior and senior year, I researched the field of college counseling. An information interview with a local college counselor helped me understand the route many took into this field.

What I found out was many college counselors started out teaching for a couple of years and completed a master's in counseling education. With the master's degree, these educators transitioned into guidance counseling at the secondary level. After many years of guidance counseling, these counselors started transitioning into college counselor/advisor roles. Once retirement was near, these counselors started offering their knowledge on a part-time basis to students and families. Another route I saw individuals take was working in college admissions as a recruiter and then transitioning to the other side: college counseling.

I decided to take the most direct path possible to my dream. I earned a master's degree in social work and sat for the licensing exam for the state of Texas. As a licensed master's level social worker (LMSW), I was formally trained in counseling and poised to bring the sensitivity of a counselor to the role of a college counselor. After carefully exploring field placement options in year two of graduate school, I was able to identify a nonprofit that operated a charter high school. This charter high school also had a college and career center for teens. Fortunately, I was able to intern in this college and career center. Weeks into my practicum, I was hired! I was one of a few graduate students in my class earning a full-time salary while I was finishing up my master's degree. A year later, I was the center's coordinator and supervising up to 10 staff. This position allowed me to gain experience working with teens in the space of career exploration, job search, and on a limited basis, college search. While I was employed there, I started my college advising business and worked this side hustle for seven years.

CHAPTER FIVE

Final Thoughts/Words

Thank you for joining me on my journey. You now know more about this first-generation college student raised by a Black working-class father determined to help his daughters succeed after his wife suddenly and unexpectedly died of a heart attack. Like so many, my life has been impacted by death, discouragement, divorce, and doubt. Throughout my life, I learned to defy the odds and to disempower limiting beliefs. You can too!

Cliff Note Highlights

Let me begin by revisiting the Cliff Note presented in this book. Below is a summary of the big takeaways in Generation EDGE:

Chapter 1

- Work through your childhood trauma. Your future self will thank you as you are able to fully embrace your destiny without baggage from your childhood.

- Sometimes your biggest weakness can become your superpower. Before you determine you are simply not good at something, work on developing that skill.

Chapter 2

- Sometimes we need someone to believe in us and the greatness that lies within. It can make a difference!

- Do not let someone else tell you what you cannot do. (English teachers, please excuse the double negatives.)

- Where there is a will, there is a way.

- What do you want? How badly do you want it?! If you want it badly enough, you can find a way to make it work. Start early. Research. Get help when you need it. Be diligent.

Chapter 3

- Listen to YOUR gut; it will help you avoid heartache and detours.

- Don't choose your career based on what others think. You are the one who has to live with the decision. Choose a career based on YOUR interests, aptitudes, and personality. Develop a career plan that takes income into consideration.

Chapter 4

- Trying different things can teach us important lessons, such as where we thrive and where we don't. Learning what isn't a fit is just as important!

- Opportunity is all around you. Sometimes it's about seeing a need and devising a way to fill it. Shortcomings can become an opportunity.

More from Dr. Jen

As I close, I would like to share some additional thoughts that may encourage you in your career and life journey. Some of these statements come from my social media, including many podcast interviews posted online. Follow me on Instagram, Twitter, Facebook, and YouTube @drjenprice for more inspiration.

Be you...and be the best version of yourself.

"I love you every day...all day...no matter what. You are my favorite [insert name] in the whole wide world. I love you because you are mine. You are a gift from God [insert name]."

Above is an excerpt from what I tell my son before bed. I tell him these things each night no matter where I am. I want him to know he is loved by me unconditionally. I want him to know the love I have for him is every day; it lasts all day, even if I get frustrated with him. I love him no matter what happens and whether he makes good or poor choices.

When I tell my son he is my favorite, it is because I want him to understand there is no one else like him in the whole world. I know this is super sappy and ooey gooey, but what would happen if you loved yourself this way? What if you realized you were a gift set here on this earth by God for others?

Because I realize I am a gift to the world, I also recognize I have an obligation to others to be the best version of myself. When I don't fully show up and give what's in me to give, others may hurt, fail, or live beneath their potential. The same is true for my son, and the same is true for you.

Be courageous...be you! Be the best version of you—others are counting on it.

Be kind to yourself.

No one is perfect. No one expects you to be perfect, so why do you?

I grew up trying to do everything right, especially in the classroom. Striving for perfection, I tried to earn all A's my entire academic career. I can still remember how devastated I was to earn that first B in 5th grade; it was an 89. I wept uncontrollably.

I wish I could say I lightened up over the years, but I didn't. Even in my doctoral program, I was determined to earn all A's. Some nights I would work through the entire night on an assignment or paper. Despite my best efforts, I earned a number of A minuses and graduated with a 3.90 on a 4.0 scale. My body somehow endured years of stress, but not without the consequences of developing hypertension and weakened relationships. Was this level of academic achievement necessary at the PhD level? No!

Pushing yourself to excel is a good thing, but not at the expense of your health and well-being.

Ask yourself "What?": What are you feeling? What do you need? Give yourself what you need. This will help you live a more satisfying life.

Being in work or study mode so much of the time, I was utterly disconnected from myself...who I was and what I felt. Despite working in a counseling-related field, I feel as though I've only recently become more self-aware. If you don't know who you are or what's going on with you, you don't know what you need. If your needs are not being met, it's difficult to enjoy your life to the fullest.

As a way to stay connected to yourself, start considering how you feel. Whether you acknowledge the feeling consciously or not, your body is reacting. That tension in your neck or stomachache represents a feeling you may not be acknowledging. The moodiness or anger you feel may be the result of you studying a major that doesn't ignite your passions or working in a job that is not a fit.

Try talking with a trusted friend, listening to music, journaling, or taking a walk to give you time to understand what is going on with you. Seeking out help can also bring you greater clarity.

Do something every day towards your dream(s).

Back when I was in high school and college, studying abroad was not as big as it is now. (This was also pre-COVID, of course). I dreamt of going to Paris, France. To work towards my dream, I took French despite living in state with many Spanish speakers. I joined the French Club and even became an officer. In college, I continued with the language and with learning about French culture.

Overtime, life kicked in. I started living life on autopilot and got caught up in boring daily tasks. Although there were certain things that need to be done (school/work, dishes, laundry, etc.), I never let go of that dream. Ten years after graduate school, I traveled to Paris with my former spouse. To my surprise, the trip activated some of what I had learned in school. The trip was well worth the wait! There is nothing like seeing the Eiffel Tower sparkling at night.

What can you do today to take steps toward realizing your dream, whatever that is?

If you don't quit, you win.

I haven't had any posts go viral yet on social media. There was one post on LinkedIn that had a ton of views though. In January of 2019, I posted a picture of me proudly fanning my $150 cash prize from my gym. I won 2nd place for the most pound, inches, and percentage of body fat lost. The numbers were significant, but not huge. To be quite frank, I think I won due to my persistence.

The contest happened around the holidays when people were likely to cheat on their diet at holiday parties and skip going to the gym to shop for gifts. I steadily maintained my gym routine and watched out for sweets.

Sometimes we win not because we are the best, but because we refuse to quit.

I encourage you to take this lesson from my late Pastor Jim Lillard to heart. It will change the outcomes in your life!

CHAPTER SIX

Resources

Below are some regional and national resources I used to help me learn more about starting a business. Find similar organizations in your area or access the same nationwide resources.

City of Austin, Small and Minority Business Resources

http://www.austintexas.gov/department/small-and-minority-business-resources-0

Small Business Association

https://www.sba.gov/

Business Invest in Growth (BiG Austin)

https://www.bigaustin.org/

Professional Women of Williamson County

https://pwownetwork.org/

SCORE

http://www.score.org

Austin Community College (ACC)

https://www.austincc.edu/

Rice Alliance

https://alliance.rice.edu/

IECA

https://www.iecaonline.com/

UCLA Extension

https://www.uclaextension.edu

Appendices

Appendix A

College Visits

The ideal time to visit a campus is when it is in session. During the academic year, students and families can see the student body and level of student-to-student interaction. There are times lectures, along with student-teacher interaction, may be observed. Food in the dining hall can also be sampled. In the summer, campuses are generally under construction and few students are on campus.

If an in-person visit is not possible, search college websites for virtual campus tours or find campus highlight videos online.

College resource guidebooks like those published by Edward Fiske or Lauren Pope (Colleges That Change Lives) offer narratives regarding the campus environment and experience.

Homework Activity

What are some good dates and times to visit colleges on your list? Take out the calendar and map out a plan with your family. Take advantage of any school holidays, especially long weekends. Familiarize yourself with the high school's policy on absences due to college visits and plan accordingly.

Remember to take pictures and take notes on each campus. Include comments on whether you can see yourself on that campus and if there are any possible areas of concern. Consider using the College Visits Tips handout from Dr. Jen Price to document your experience. Keep all your notes together in one place, possibly in a binder or in a journal.

Campus Visit Checklist

Name of School:
_____

Date of Visit:
_____

Tour Guide Name:
_____

General Planning Tips:

- Plan to spend at least a half-day on campus. If possible, stay overnight to see and accomplish everything on your checklist.

- Visit when the college or university is in session (i.e., fall or spring).

- Consider picking a day to visit when there is also an extracurricular event to participate in (i.e., sports, theatre, etc.) to get a taste of the student experience.

Before the Visit:

- Register for an admissions information session and campus tour.

- Contact the admissions officer for your region to see if you can visit a class in the major you are considering.

- If you have questions, schedule an appointment with a financial aid officer.

- Schedule an appointment with an academic advisor in the major you are considering if you have questions.

- If you are hoping to play college-level sports, schedule an appointment with a coach.

What to Wear/Bring:

- Comfortable walking shoes

- Sunscreen (if needed)

- Backpack (for journal and pen, bottled water, snacks, etc.)

- Journal and pen to take notes (i.e., contacts, questions, observations, action items) or jot down notes in your cell phone

- Questions already written down for each department or person you are visiting

- Bottled water and non-temperature sensitive snacks (i.e., peanut butter crackers, granola bars, etc.)

- Credit card and cash for meals or parking

While You're on Campus:

- Tour the campus
- Meet with an admissions officer
- Meet with an academic advisor
- Sit in on a class in your major
- Meet with a financial aid officer
- Meet with a coach if you hope to compete in athletics at the college level
- Visit the housing office to pick up information about dorms or apartments and take a tour
- Check out the Student Union, bookstore, and libraries (notice what ATMs are on campus and where they are located; notice what kind of supplies/items are available on campus in case of emergencies)
- Visit departmental or university-wide career center(s) to see what services are available to students, especially job placement assistance during college and after graduation
- Pick up a student newspaper or activities calendar

- Drive around the community surrounding the campus

List your schedule for the day below. Include names, numbers, and building locations. Print out any confirmations for your visit and attach it to this handout packet.

_____

_____

_____

_____

_____

_____

_____

_____

_____

_____

_____

_____

_____

_____

Questions to Ask:

Tour Guide

Ask the guide for a campus map and for help marking where your appointments are for the day.

- Support Services
    - What tutoring, counseling, and support services are available on campus and how are they accessed? What are the fees for accessing these services?
    - Where are the computer labs on campus? What kind of computer access will students have? Are laptops required?
- Campus Activities
    - Ask them where to find out about campus activities.

- o What activities do students participate in during their free time on campus (school sponsored) and in the community?

- o What are the most popular extracurricular activities?

- Transportation/Parking Issues

  - o Can freshman have cars on campus? What kind of fees are associated with having a car on campus?

  - o What transportation options are available to and from campus for trips to discount stores and transportation centers (e.g., airports, bus and train stations)?

- Miscellaneous

  - o What are the most controversial issues on campus?

Admissions

- What does the college consider in the admissions process: courses, grades, test scores, rank, interests, institutional needs, essays, recommendations, and interviews? How important are these factors?

- Which academic programs are most popular? Which are the hardest to get into?

- What are the largest classes a freshman might have? How many large classes are there? Who teaches them: professors or teaching/graduate assistants?

- If applicable, what kind of assistance is available for students needing additional support in the classroom or for testing due to ADD, ADHD, LD, etc.?

- (If interested) Ask if there is an Honors Program and how does one qualify for it. Are there any benefits associated with participation in an honors program (e.g., scholarships, special housing, etc.)?

Academic Advisor

- Ask the advisor for a copy of your degree plan.

- Are students able to graduate in four years? What kind of support is in place to promote graduation in four years?

- Can they show you around the building where your major is housed or direct you to the appropriate building?

- Are there any departmental scholarships, especially for incoming freshman?

- Is there a career center for this department? What type of services does it offer? Where is it?

Financial Aid Officer

- What is the yearly cost of attendance, including housing, meal plans, books, and tuition? In other words, what is the full cost of attendance?

- Which financial aid forms are required? (The most common forms are FAFSA and the CSS PROFILE, but some schools have institutional or school specific forms.)

- What percentage of entering freshmen receive aid? What was the average freshman aid package? How much of the package were grants or scholarships? Loans?

- How do students find out about work-study or on-campus employment opportunities?

Housing and Food Services

- What percentage of the student body lives on campus? What percentage of the student body stays off campus?

- What portion of the student body stays on campus during the weekends?

- Is campus housing guaranteed for all four years?

- What housing options exist? (Honors housing? Single sex? Co-ed? Greek? Theme housing?)

- What meal plans are available? Are freshmen required to purchase a specific type of meal plan? Does the cafeteria offer gluten-free, vegetarian/vegan, and or dairy-free options?

- What hours may students access food services? Are there limited hours on the weekend?

- How much is the housing deposit?

- How are roommates assigned?

- Where are the laundry facilities? Do the machines accept credit cards and/or text you when your load is complete?

- What are the safety issues on campus? How are they addressed? Ask for a crime report or for where you might be able to find one. (Federal law requires schools to provide safety information to students.)

If a person doesn't have an answer, ask them who might be able to answer the question.

Current or past students are also great resources.

Appendix B

Sample Resumes

Sample Resume #1

IMMA GIRL

immagirl@gmail.com

OBJECTIVE

To attend a widely credited college or university.

EDUCATION

- Central Texas High School (Distinguished Achievement Graduate)
- Anticipated Graduation Date May 2021

- Unweighted GPA: 98.6920
- Class Rank: 7 (out of 509)
- AP (4) and Pre-AP (9) Classes

WORK EXPERIENCE

2015-Present   The Smith Family   Austin, TX

Babysitter

- Cared for 3 boys (ages 1, 3, 5)
- Played indoor and outdoor games

2014-Present   Pets Across America (CPAA)   Austin, TX

Co-founder (summers only)

- Created a non-profit organization
- Raised money by pet sitting, house sitting, and walking dogs
- Donated profits to area social service

VOLUNTEER

- Tutoring peers in math and science (2019-Present)

- Assisted in El Buen Samaritano Child Center (2018-2020)

- Raised money for Salvation Army: Angel Tree (2015-2018)

EXTRACURRICULAR

2014-Present   Choir   Austin, TX

Central Texas's Freshmen, Varsity Women, and Choral Choir Groups

- Solo and Ensemble Outstanding Choir Award (2016-Present)

- School Musical (2019-Present)

- Voice Lessons (2017-Present)

- Choir Secretary (2018-2020)

2001-2008	Women's Soccer	Austin, TX

Club Soccer (2014-Present)

- Super Blue and Division I Player
- Team Captain (2014-2016 and 2018-Present)

Central Texas High School Soccer Team (2018-Present)

- Earned Women's Varsity position

2015-Present	Destination Imagination (DI)	Austin, TX

- Designed and performed improvisational skits
- Developed and demonstrated problem solving skills
- Improved leadership, communication, and teamwork skill

2019-Present	Mu Alpha Theta Club	Austin, TX
2019-Present	Spanish Club	Austin, TX
2019-2020	Model United Nations Club	Austin, TX
2020-Present	Chemistry Club	Austin, TX
2020-Present	National Honor Society	Austin, TX

AWARDS

Student of the Year Awards

- English, Math, Biology (2018-2019)
- English, Chemistry, World History, Spanish (2019-2020)

Destination Imagination (DI)

- Spirit of DI Award (2019)
- Renaissance Award (2020)
- DaVinci Award (2019)
- 2nd place (2017, 2018, 2019)
- 1st place (2020)

Outstanding Student Choir Award (2019)

Soccer

- Academic All-District (2019, 2020)
- Club Soccer 4th in State (2019)

- School Soccer: 2019 District 16 Champions, 2019 Region 2 Semi-Finalists, 2020 District 25 Champions, 2020 Region 4 Champions, 2020 5A State Semi-Finalists

Sample Resume #2

I.S. Aboy

Email: isaboy@gmail.com Phone: (828) XXX-XXXX

OBJECTIVE

To obtain admission to a university that will sufficiently prepare me for my future.

EDUCATION

2017-Present   Hut High School   Brevard, NC

- 4.205 GPA on a 5.0 scale
- Class rank in the top 10%
- Graduation June 2020

EXTRACURRICULAR ACTIVITIES

2017-Present	Hut High School Football Team	Brevard, NC

Quarterback/Wide Receiver/Defensive Back

- Helped lead team to district championship freshman year (2017)
- Selected offensive MVP on junior varsity team in 2018
- Awarded Academic All-District patch in 2019
- Set all-time school record for number of interceptions in one game (3) 2019
- Invited to be a member of the Senior Leadership Council 2020

2017-Present	Hut High School Basketball Team	Brevard, NC

Point/Shooting Guard

- Started on a co-district champion freshman team
- Acquired a full-time starting position on the varsity team 2018-2019
- Received Academic and Honorable Mention all-district honors 2018-2019

- Elected to the All-District team and academic all-district 2019-2020

2017-2018   Hut High School   Brevard, NC
                  Track Team

800m/1600 m Runner

- Placed 1st in the Lexington Eagle Relays in both 800m and 1600 m races

- Won the gold medal in the district track meet in the 1600m run and silver in the 800 m run

WORK EXPERIENCE

2019-Present   YMCA   Brevard, NC

Summer Camp Counselor

- Supervised children ages 5-12

- Facilitated recreational activities such as basketball and archery

Summer 2019   Family Swim Gym   Brevard, NC

Lifeguard

- Elected lifeguard of the month at Blackhawk Amenity Center June 2019
- Certified in lifeguarding, first aide, and AED use
- Enforced safe behavior at all times
- Oversaw residents swimming in Blackhawk Community Pool

COMMUNITY SERVICE

- Aided in planting many donated palm trees in a new neighborhood (5 hrs)
- Timed and congratulated Special Olympics participants (4 hrs)
- Helped run a community washers tournament and clean up Town Square afterwards (4 hrs)
- Coached a youth soccer league team of 5 to 6-year-olds (35 hrs)
- Assisted in running the YMCA Halloween Carnival (3 hrs)

ACADEMIC HONORS

- Selected to attend Herff Jones Student Leadership Convention 2020

- Chosen to be a member of the National Society of High School Scholars 2018

- Voted Most Creative Writer in Freshman English 2017

Sample Resume #3

Moore Girl

1235 Noname Lane

Orange, CA 90620   (562) XXX-XXXX

Noname@gmail.com

OBJECTIVE

To gain entrance into a competitive university.

EDUCATION

2015-Present	Wood High School	Orange, CA

- Graduated June 2019 on Distinguished Plan.
- 3.845 GPA (weighted)/3.3 GPA (unweighted)

Summer 2017 & 2018	Orange Community College	Orange, CA

- Completed Government and Economics in the summer of 2018

- Completed Speech and Health in the summer of 2017

- Was awarded Advanced Measures for getting a B or higher toward high school graduation plan for three of the classes

VOLUNTEER EXPERIENCE

2006-Present   Girl Scouts of the USA   Orange, CA

Daisy through Senior

- Managed Twilight Camp, a yearly summer camp for approximately 80 girls in elementary school

- Taught lessons on animals, movies, plays, and outdoor cooking

- Planned at least 20 camping trips, i.e., Camp Lake, Camp Kachina, and Falls State Park

- Helped plan a meeting for troop of 10 girls at least four times a year

- Created and delivered handmade crafts to the elderly participating in the Meals on Wheels program
- Introduced 50 girls (kindergarten through fifth grade) to the Girl Scout Handbook alongside an adult leader

2017-Present	Girls Giving Grants	Orange, CA

Treasurer (2018-19); Member (2017-18)

- Collect and deposit fees from approximately 60 teen girls
- Evaluate 5 applications from Orange-area nonprofits and vote to select the grant recipient

WORK EXPERIENCE

2018-Present	Baskin Robbins	Orange, CA

Team Member

- Prepare ice cream, frozen yogurt, and frozen treats for sale
- Collect payment

- Clean store as needed and finish daily list of chores

2017-2018　　　　City of Orange　　　Orange, CA

Crossing Guard

- Stopped traffic to allow children and parents to cross safely

- Attended two hours of training

Summer 2017　　　　Randall's Grocery　　　Orange, CA

Cashier

- Provided customers with "World Class Service," a technique only Randall's uses to treat customers with great service

- Kept my station clean and organized to be efficient

Summers 2010-2016　　Baker's Dozen　　　Orange, CA
　　　　　　　　　　　Breads

Intern

- Maintained the organization of the store (cleaning, stocking)

- Baked cookies and cakes

- Built customer relationships through welcome greetings and recommendations for products
- Helped with children's summer classes which included teaching weaving, sewing, or cooking

EXTRACURRICULAR ACTIVITIES

2017-Present   Wood Dancers   Orange, CA

Team Member (2018-19); Manager (2017-18)

- As a manager:
    - Helped prepare and attended practices for our yearly spring show, Escapade
    - Attended at least four competitions in which our team won multiple awards
    - Helped with the competition we hosted at our school

2015-2017   Wood Choir   Orange, CA

Varsity Choir (2016-17); Women's Choir (2015-16)

- Sung in the Soprano I section

- Had a minimum of three concerts per year
- Performed Cabaret, our largest concert which included skits, solos, small ensembles and large group performances, each February
- Prepared and participated in the yearly UIL contests

AWARDS

Girl Scouts of the USA Orange, CA

Silver Award

- Provided premature babies with blankets through Threads of Love
- Created the warp for the blankets and wove them on a loom
- Sewed the edges of the blankets and delivered them to Threads of Love

Contemporary Handweavers Orange, CA

Third place in the Children's Division

- Wove three towels containing organic fibers on a loom

- Attended the convention at the Airport Hilton in Orange
- Entered three towels in the Children's Division

References

"Alignment." Merriam-Webster.com Dictionary, Merriam-Webster, https://www.merriam-webster.com/dictionary/alignment. Accessed 29 Aug. 2020.

"ASCA Releases Updated Student-to-School-Counselor Ratio Data." *American School Counselor Association*, American School Counselor Association, 14 Apr. 2020, www.schoolcounselor.org/asca/media/asca/Press%20releases/PR_18-19Student-to-SC-Ratios.pdf.

Acknowledgments

First, I want to thank God for His faithfulness. You never stopped loving me or pursuing me, even when I was angry and didn't understand what was happening in my life. It took some time, but I ultimately saw you were not the one who caused the pain. You were the one sending support and direction during the pain. Often, the help came in unexpected ways and packages. Thank you.

Again, I want to thank my family. Momma, although we were only together the first seven years of my life, I am grateful to have had a chance to know you and to experience a mother's love. Thank you for passing on that ambition and sense of style. Because of you and Daddy, I love books and learning. Daddy, we butted heads often because of our different worldviews, but I know without a doubt you loved me. Thank you for providing a stable and peaceful home environment. I appreciate all the times you washed the dishes so I could do my schoolwork. Your confidence in me laid a foundation in me that can never be taken away; I know I can do anything I set my mind to. You showed me good men do exist, so I was able to avoid a whole lot of foolishness and to focus on my education and career. Thank you for teaching me about money through your example. Because I learned about financial stewardship early, I was again able to avoid many pitfalls and was prepared to pursue my dream. Thank you!

I am thankful that my sisters, Holly Rivers, Kimberly Houston, and Jessica Taylor, are still on this earth with me. We are what is left of our immediate family. I appreciate the times we have been able to give one another support. We may not see eye to eye on every issue, but I love each of you and am proud of each one of you and of your successes to date. Holly, it's been fun seeing our children grow up together and how close they've become.

I want to acknowledge my son. Son, your father and I endured much to see your arrival, but we are eternally grateful for your presence in our lives. I wasn't able to grow up with a mom, so I am doing everything I can to stay here on this earth to pour into you and to watch you grow and mature. Thank you for your unconditional love, especially all the hugs and smiles. You are truly a gift from God.

Thank you to my extended family and friends who loved on me, especially during my times of brokenness. When many fell away, I learned who really loved me. I am especially grateful for Rashona Thomas, Crystal Arthur, Haja Iscandri Scott, Shirley Thomas, Yolanda Bellesen Adams, Yvette Gauff and my childhood friends who have always been there: Tien Koehler, Margarita de la Garza, Amy Byrne Morreale, and Amy Griggs. I thank Pastor Eric and Andrea

Moore of Summit Worship Center for operating a church that extends graces, pours out love, and promotes community. I am grateful for the healing that has taken place in me since I started attending Summit (live and online). The messages are relevant and challenge me to grow. Plus, the praise and worship is amazing!

There have also been important mentors in my life ranging from my 2nd grade teacher to present. After my mother died, an elementary teacher, Mrs. Dale Cook, continued to encourage my interest in reading. I will never forget the Strawberry Shortcake Doll you bought me as a reward for reading the most books in my class or the $50 check you sent me upon graduating high school. Your extra attention meant the world to me. In high school, Coach Laura Schmidt pushed me as a runner, but she knew academics would take me further. Thank you for nominating me for the Conroe High Sportswoman of the Year award in 1992. At that time, I needed the recognition.

I am eternally grateful to Howard and Nancy Terry of the Terry Foundation. Because of their generousness, I was able to attend The University of Texas at Austin on a full-ride academic scholarship.

Thank you to the many students and families I have served in the classroom, counselor's office, and in my private practice. I appreciate your trust and confidence in sharing your disappointment and dreams. It has truly been an honor to help you map out plans for college and career success.

In the professional realm, I have been blessed to receive inspiration and guidance from many mentors. Thank you to my late Pastor Jim Lillard, Brendon Burchard's Millionaire Messenger and conferences, Coach and Counselor Sonya Jensen, Business Success Coach Oginga Carr, Author Brian Johnson and Best Seller Accelerator peers, Relationship/Business Coach and Author Tony Gaskins, and my local independent educational consultants affinity group.

I would also like to acknowledge those who have helped me with my business at different phases: the staff of Spicewood Professional Offices, Anitra Hendricks, Vatina Robinson, and Asha Petrich.

So many more have helped me impact teens, young adults, and their families over the years, and my thanks go out to them as well. I appreciate you.

Thank you in advance to others I will encounter in this journey to inspire, educate, and empower others.

About the Author

For over 20 years, UVISEME's (You-vize-me) Founder Jenifer Price, PhD, LMSW has offered strategic advice to high school, early career adults, and their families in the college and career selection process. She has visited 200+ colleges nationwide and has helped students collectively win over $15 million dollars in scholarships to date.

Dr. Jen is not only a college and career coach, but she is an author, speaker, and online course creator. Her guidance minimizes the confusion and stress associated with college admissions, lowers the cost of attendance, promotes more timely graduation rates, and increases career satisfaction.

She helps students and families in a number of ways: through her book *Generation E.D.G.E.: The Student's 4-Step Guide to College & Career Success*, her online course College EDGE (mycollegeedge.com), and one-on-one coaching.

Dr. Jen's son inspires her to do and be the best version of herself each day.

Also by Dr. Jen Price, LMSW

Online Course

College Edge (mycollegeedge.com),

an online college advising course for students and families

grades 7th-12th

Seminars/Speeches by Dr. Jen Price, LMSW:

How to Make Your Student's Dream College a Reality

What Failing at Organic Chemistry Taught Me

Meet Dr. Jen Price, LMSW online and receive free resources at

www.drjenprice.com

www.ingramcontent.com/pod-product-compliance
Lightning Source LLC
Chambersburg PA
CBHW050648160426
43194CB00010B/1852